HELL IS NOT IN CHARGE

HELL IS NOT IN CHARGE

By

Dr. Johnny Burrell

IPC
I.T.N.O.J. Publishing Consultants
PO Box 2265
Clarksville, TN 37042
www.lmcneeseministries.org

Cover Design by Simone Cuarino

Copyright 2005

All rights reserved. No part of this book may be reproduced in any form, except for the inclusion of brief quotations in a review, without permission in writing from its publisher or the author.

Take note that the name satan and related names are not capitalized. We choose not to acknowledge him, even to the point of violating grammatical rules.

Library of Congress Control Number:

2005909332

ISBN 0-9761490-1-X

Printed in the United States by

Morris Publishing
Kearney, NE

ଔ Dedication ଓ

To my wife Lucille

Although the life of an Apostolic First Lady can at times seem lonely, unrewarding and quite difficult; you have laughed with me, cried with me, loved, stayed and prayed with me through sickness and health, for better, for worse for 42 years.

Your price is far above rubies.

❧ Acknowledgements ☙

I don't know where I would be if God had not given me faithful friends and supporters such as …

Mr. & Mrs. James Williams
Mr. & Mrs. Oscar Booker
Mr. & Mrs. Larry Sanders
Mr. & Ms. Ephraim Kenner
Mr. & Ms. William Carr
Mr. & Ms. Marion Sanders
Mr. & Ms. Kevin Colbert
Hattie Green
Helen Drake
Mattie Booker
Kevin Colbert & Family
Amos Cowan & Family
Ms. Bertha Core
Linda Smith
My sons Gregory and Reginald Burrell and their wives.
Mr. & Mrs. Kay Graham
My daughter Regina & husband, Dr. Joseph Grant
and
The Pentecostal Lighthouse Church Family.

ॐ **Special Thanks** ☙

To Atnea, Helen and the entire congregation of the *Pentecostal Lighthouse* for inspiring this work.
To my friend and publisher, L. McNeese, who believed in this project from day one and would not allow anything to hinder it.
And most importantly, to my Lord and Savior Jesus Christ that took the keys from the devil on our behalf so that we can rightly say that

Hell is not in charge!

TABLE OF CONTENTS

Foreword 10

Chapter I
What is Hell? 13

Chapter II
What Does Hell Want? 23

Chapter III
Myths, Facts and Folly on Hell 36

Chapter IV
The Skinny on satan 45

Chapter V
Behind the Smoke and Mirrors 60

Chapter VI
satan's Devices 69

Chapter VII
The Greatest Lies ever Told 84

Chapter VIII
Top 10 Reasons Hell is not in Charge 92

Chapter IX
How To Be Delivered 97

Chapter X
Who's in Charge? 102

Glossary 110

Bibliography 115

"Behold, I give unto you power to tread on serpents and scorpions, and over all the power of the enemy: and nothing shall by any means hurt you."

Luke 10:19

ॐ FOREWORD ॐ

According to a gallop poll taken in the 90s only about 60% of the American population believes in hell. If correct, this means that 40% of Americans alone have fallen for one of satan's biggest schemes. For more information on his biggest lies, see chapter seven. The world with its population of billions is not only headed for a close encounter with the anti-Christ, but an afterlife of torment that for many will be no surprise. Statistics have shown that even some of those who call themselves born-again Christians deny the existence of hell.

C.S. Lewis once said that he had never met a person who did not believe in hell and also fully believe in heaven. In other words, when people say that hell is not real they usually start doubting if heaven is real. It is unclear why people deny the existence of hell. Many point out the world's condition as a reason for their denial. Little kids are born diseased and deformed, Tsunami, tornados and wars destroy the lives and livelihoods of millions each year. Countries are suffering from famine and poverty. Some say: "If there were a God he wouldn't allow these things to occur." Others quip: "I know I'm going to heaven because I've done my time in hell."

These ideas, statements and attitudes all give power to satan and further the reign of control and wickedness that he has on the earth. The anti-hell attitude has even crept into the church. While devout Christians do not usually outright deny the existence of satan, petty fears and problems often overcome the victorious life that Christ died to ensure for them. Has the devil stolen your joy? Are you losing control? The Bible tells us that the thief cometh not but to steal, kill and destroy, but Christ also came that we might have life.

Hell is not in Charge is written in an effort to expose the father of lies (satan) and to encourage every child of God to charge into the enemy's camp and get back all that he has stolen. In the face of the devil's opposition God wants you to know where the real power lies. Keys are important; they can give you freedom, protect your valuables or represent your power. Those who are imprisoned long for a key, those who are confused search for keys to understanding. Whoever holds the key also holds access to blessings. Jesus took the keys of death and hell from the devil on our behalf so that no matter what comes our way, be it pain, pestilence, famine or any other of satan's tools, we can stand up, square our shoulders, rebuke the adversary and testify with confidence that ***Hell is not in Charge!***

"I am he that liveth, and was dead; and, behold, I am alive for evermore, Amen; and have the keys of hell and death."

Rev. 1:18

Dr. Johnny Burrell

Chapter I

WHAT IS HELL?

Despite various "educated" and ignorant attempts to deny the existence of hell, testimonies of men and God (through his word) still bear witness of the fact that there is a definite place of evil for those who dwell outside of the will of God. For Richard Bach hell is a place, a time, a consciousness in which there is no love. Oscar Wilde quipped: "We are all our own devil and we make this world our hell." Whether you agree with these writers or not there is no mistaking what the Bible says concerning the punishment and eternal nature of hell:

1. The wicked end up in hell with the devil and his angels. Matt. 25:41

2. Jesus said that the fire there is unquenchable. Mark 9:43

3. There is weeping and gnashing of teeth in hell. Matt. 8:12

4. There is no hope in Hell. Luke 16:26

These are just a few of the many mentions by men and God about hell. It must be remembered that a man only becomes wise when he begins to calculate the depth of his ignorance. Man's disbelief in hell will not make this horrible condition and reality go away. Rather than foolishly denying hell's existence man would do better by trying to understand where and what hell really is.

The word "hell" is most commonly used in these ways:

1. As a reference to a netherworld in which the dead continue to live and suffer.
2. As a slang expression of anger, annoyance or disappointment.
3. Any place, situation or condition of trouble and suffering.
4. The powers of evil.

For the sake of understanding the word "hell" in the title of this book, *"Hell is not in Charge"* refers to the latter two. Hence, another way to say that hell is not in charge is to say that **the powers of evil are not in control** or **the situation that the**

powers of evil have brought into your life cannot run your life (not in charge). A clearly combined definition is this: As a child of God neither satan, his imps, nor the pain and problems that they present is going to dictate the way my life will go. Hell is not in charge!

There is nothing in the Bible uglier than hell: not Judas' kiss of betrayal, not Jezebel's blood stained hands, not the murderous voice of Cain telling God a suggestive lie ("Am I my brother's keeper?"). The word "hell" is the icon for an ugly place, a place of pain, a place of trouble. Jesus spoke of hell in a long and emotional discourse that made listeners certainly want to avoid it at all cost.

"... the rich man also died, and was buried; And in hell he lifted up his eyes, being in torments, ..."
Luke 16:22b & 23a

As discussed earlier, hell is both a condition and a territory. Hell is the evil brought about by the forces of darkness.

As a territory hell appears in holy writ as the beginning of an eternal life of torment, but the afterlife is not of much concern to those who are saved and sanctified. We who have given our lives to the Lord and are walking in the light of holiness do not have to worry about the so-called devil's hell that awaits them that live in sin. The enemy knows this and since we are not going to hell, he has decided to bring hell to us! There has been considerable debate among so called scholars as to the duration of punishment in hell. Some teach that hell is purgatorial and that the suffering is temporary, designed to purge us clean while our living relatives pray us out of the purgatorial fire. Others have taught that the length of punishment in hell will be equal to the guilt of an individual hellion. Obviously, the Bible does not agree with these ideas, but when hell brings its evil to us, how long does it last? How long should it last? Does hell (satan) decide how long we suffer or does God have a predetermined time? The Bible gives us clues, but there is one in particular that actually happens every day. It is found in the book of Jonah. This book (Jonah) is about salvation. The salvation of Jonah, the salvation of the heathens of a town called Nineveh, and the physical deliverance from what Jonah calls the belly of <u>hell</u>!

Jonah chapter 2:

1   Then Jonah prayed unto the Lord his God out of the fish's belly,

2   And said, I cried by reason of mine affliction unto the Lord, and he heard me; out of the belly of hell cried I, and thou heardest my voice.

3   For thou hadst cast me into the deep, in the midst of the seas; and the floods compassed me about: all thy billows and thy waves passed over me.

4   Then said I, I am cast out of thy sight; yet I will look again toward thy holy temple.

5   The waters compassed me about, even to the soul: the depth closed me round about, the weeds were wrapped about my head.

6   I went down to the bottoms of the mountains; the earth with her bars was about me for ever: yet hast

thou brought up my life from corruption, O Lord my God.

7 When my soul fainted within me I remembered the Lord: and my prayer came in unto thee, into thine holy temple.

8 They that observe lying vanities forsake their own mercy.

9 But I will sacrifice unto thee with the voice of thanksgiving; I will pay that that I have vowed. Salvation is of the Lord.

10 And the Lord spake unto the fish, and it vomited out Jonah upon the dry land.

Since this is such a familiar story, I'll sum it up for you: Jonah was a great prophet, but he decided to go in a direction that God had not ordained. The number one cause of pain, evil and trouble on earth is men deciding to do contrary to what God has said.

Next, we find Jonah asleep on a ship unaware that a great storm had moved out over the ocean. Most of the trouble (hell) that we go through could have been lessened if we had awakened out of our sleep of comfort and complacency and dealt with pesky demons early on. Next, the story of Jonah tells us that even the pagan sailors were praying while Jonah was asleep. How long will our righteousness not exceed that of the scribes and Pharisees? Next, we see Jonah wake up, get up and end up down deep in hell – trouble, pain, anguish! He was going through because he heard God and either ignored or avoided God's holy word! How long did Jonah have to go through this trouble? Only until he decided to repent unto God and recognize that God's way was the best way. What is hell (for a child of God) but a temporary time of trouble? Is it not a time that can be lengthened, shortened or avoided all together if we would accept God's word as the authority in our lives and run with it?

"Hell begins on the day when God grants us a clearer vision of all that we might have achieved, of all the gifts which we have wasted, of all that we might have done which we did not do."

Gian Carlo Menotti

"Readers are advised to remember that the devil is a liar."

C.S. Lewis

(The Screwtape Letters)

Chapter II

WHAT DOES HELL WANT?

If hell were asked what it wants, the answer would be simple like Uncle Sam back in the days of the world wars and Vietnam. Hell would simply retort: "I want you!"

That is, of course, if you are a child of God and living a life of holiness. Hell doesn't need or care for its own. Those who lie, cheat, steal, curse and sin with little regard to how God feels are already citizens of hell. The greatest victory that the forces of evil can boast in is the backsliding of God's children. When a person who has committed his or her life to the Lord decides to walk in darkness, the opposite of the following text becomes true:

"Then drew near unto him all the publicans and sinners for to hear him. And the Pharisees and scribes murmured, saying, This man receiveth sinners, and eateth with them. And he spake this parable unto them, saying, What man of you, having an hundred sheep, if he lose one of them, doth not leave the ninety and nine in the wilderness, and go after that which is lost, until he find it? And when he hath found it, he layeth it on his shoulders,

rejoicing. And when he cometh home, he calleth together his friends and neighbors, saying unto them, Rejoice with me; for I have found my sheep which was lost. I say unto you, that likewise joy shall be in heaven over one sinner that repenteth, more than over ninety and nine just persons, which need no repentance." Luke 15:1-7

Unlike many of us today, Jesus knew the importance of spending time with sinners. He understood the value of a soul in the sight of God. Also, known to Jesus was the intensity with which angels looked at the human family. Angels know the seriousness of sin and the consequences that follow. They do not know from experience, but they do have a clear intellectual understanding. When the publicans and sinners drew near, Jesus did not turn them away, criticize their dress or attempt to ridicule them. He simply spoke anointed words in an effort to teach them. To do otherwise would have been exactly what hell wanted him to do. Further, Jesus was not pressured by the scribes and Pharisees into shunning those in need of salvation.

As they murmured, Jesus either read their thoughts or heard their complaints and responded with wisdom. Just as you would go into the wilderness to save one of your sheep and celebrate afterwards with your friends, God, the angels along with the host of heaven rejoices over one sinner that repents. Hell wanted that sinner, but because Jesus went into the wilderness to save him God received the glory.

What does hell want? Rejoicing, demons dance when we fail to reach out to sinners. Imps laugh when we reject sinners because of doctrinal mandates. Hell rejoices over one Christian that backslides more than over ninety-nine everyday sinners. Hell would also like to reverse every natural blessing and ounce of authority that God has given to the people of God. By natural (blessings) I am referring to any and every thing that God gave to man whether literal or symbolic. This may sound a bit extreme, but you must remember that the forces of evil are ruthless, radical and psychotic.

In Genesis we are told all that God gave to man including his instruction:

"And God blessed them, and God said unto them, Be fruitful, and multiply, and replenish the earth, and subdue it: and have dominion over the fish of the sea, and over the fowl of the air, and over every living thing that moveth upon the earth. And God said, Behold, I have given you every herb bearing seed, which is upon the face of all the earth, and every tree, in the which is the fruit of a tree yielding seed; to you it shall be for meat. And to every beast of the earth, and to every fowl of the air, and to everything that creepeth upon the earth, wherein there is life, I have given every green herb for meat: and it was so. And God saw everything that he had made, and, behold, it was very good. And the evening and the morning were the sixth day."

Gen. 1:28-31

In Gen. 1:3

He gave man light which is also figurative for knowledge.

In Gen. 1:4

God divided light from darkness which is figurative for understanding.

In Gen. 1:5

God created what amounted to day and night, giving man the gift of time.

In Gen. 1:10

God introduced the sea to man for its future benefits of food, water and travel.

In Gen. 1:11

God gave an endless blessing of replenishing seeds of grass and fruit for food.

In Gen. 1:14

God gave seasons and signs for knowledge of how to control, especially control of nature.

In Gen. 1:16

Stars were given for man's mental amusement and dreams of reaching.

In Gen. 1:20-21

God gave a diversity of birds, foul, sea creatures, all individual one from another.

In Gen. 1:25

God gave man (of the future) land animals for work, clothing, food, etc.

In Gen. 1:28

He gave man dominion.

In Gen. 2:3

God gave man a Sabbath reference to rest and take a break from his labor.

In Gen. 2:6

God gave man rain. Fresh water is symbolic of the spirit of God.

In Gen. 2:7

We notice that God had created all of the above before he even had a man to give it to. This lets us know that He is a God that always has a plan. He then gave man life and confidence that His God was a provider.

In Gen. 2:8

He gave man a home.

In Gen. 2:15

He gave man a job.

In Gen. 2:16, 17

He gave man a standard.

In Gen. 2:21-23

He gave man a family.

Now, all these blessings were good, but the forces of evil were watching the entire process and it, (hell) was angry and even jealous. He had lost his standing in the kingdom of God and could not bear to see this creature made from dust take his rightful place (in charge) of a beautiful recreated earth.

"Now the serpent was more subtle than any beast of the field which the Lord God had made. And he said unto the woman, Yea, hath God said, Ye shall not eat of every tree of the garden? And the woman said unto the serpent, We may eat of the fruit of the trees of the garden: But of the fruit of the tree which is in the midst of the garden, God hath said, Ye shall not eat of it, neither shall ye touch it, lest ye die. And the serpent said unto the woman, Ye shall not surely die:" Gen. 3:1-4

Having seen what God had blessed the man with, this vile, jealous, psychotic, sacrilegious spirit saw what it wanted, devised a plan and successfully (albeit temporarily) stripped the man of every blessing that God had given.

"So he drove out the man; and he placed at the east of the garden of Eden Cherubims, and a flaming sword which turned every way, to keep the way of the tree of life."

Gen. 3:24

So what does hell want? You and everything that is good in you. Hell wants to raise a little Cain in every peaceful moment that you attempt to enjoy. The forces of evil want to dominate your entire being to include your knowledge, your understanding, your time, your food, your car, your savings, your self control, your dreams, your individuality, your Sabbath (worship day), your health. Hell wants to drain the Spirit of God from your being and destroy your confidence, make you lose your home, job and family. All in hopes that you will lose confidence in God and lose your mind! Hell wants you dead (!) and is quite confident in her ability to get you!

> *"Therefore hell hath enlarged herself, and opened her mouth without measure: and their glory, and their multitude, and their pomp, and he that rejoiceth, shall descend into it."*
> Isa. 5:14

He is subtle and wants to employ a subconscious loss of power behind your back, but although your enemy is trying hard to drain you of the natural and spiritual joy (and energy) that God has instilled in you, you must remember that ...

> *"Ye are of God, little children, and have overcome them: because greater is he that is in you, than he that is in the world."*
> 1 John 4:4

Avoid the works of the flesh:

This is a quick explanation of these fleshly terms. For a more in-depth study you may contact my ministry office or take your time and research them yourself.

1. <u>Adultery</u> – Unfair, unlawful sexual intercourse with the spouse of another

2. <u>Fornication</u> – Illicit sexual intercourse, including adultery

3. <u>Uncleanness</u> – Unclean, impure, obscene, defiled, not sanctified to God, including acts of beastiality, lesbianism, homosexuality

4. <u>Lasciviousness</u> – Expressed lust to promote or project illicit unlawful sex and denotes excess, absence of restraint, indecency, wantonness

5. <u>Idolatry</u> – To worship or regard a person or thing above God through excessive attachment, praise with no heart-felt reverence towards God as being supreme

6. <u>Witchcraft</u> – Sorcery commonly associated with, incantations, roots and zodiacs including castings spells by medicine, potions, etc. whether the spell is good or bad in order to usurp authority or control by

manipulation

7. <u>Hatred</u> – Malicious and unjustifiable feelings towards others, whether towards the innocent or by mutual animosity.

8. <u>Variance</u> – Dissention, disputes, debating, argumentative, differing opinions.

9. <u>Emulation</u> – Of or related to jealousy that causes one to try to excel or outclass.

10. <u>Wrath</u> – Violently expressed anger.

11. <u>Strife</u> – Disputes, angry contentious attitudes toward attempts to pay back the wrong that has been inflicted.

12. <u>Seditions</u> – Rebellion against lawful authority.

13. <u>Heresies</u> – Refers to a doctrinal view that has been accepted by the people and is most used when sound doctrine is rejected and another teaching is followed.

14. <u>Envyings</u> – To resent or look upon another grudgingly because of their superiority.

15. <u>Murders</u> – To kill, including to spoil or injure the happiness of another.

16. <u>Drunkenness</u> – A state of dizziness, resulting from drinking alcoholic beverages.

17. <u>Revellings</u> – Lascivious, boisterous, feasting and partying with loud music, etc.

18. <u>Jealousy</u> – A feeling or state of suspicions rivalry coupled with envy; to be careful, watchful and to demand exclusive loyalty.

These are the things that hell wants (in you).

Don't be deceived, stand up and let the enemy know that **Hell is not in Charge!**

Chapter III

MYTHS, FACTS AND FOLLY ON HELL

FACT:

If you live right
heaven belongs to you.

Despite the many jokes about hell, insulting phrases that include the word hell and so many people in danger of going to hell, most people are still quite under informed about the *place* called hell. There are also many myths about hell that have surfaced over the years due to the casual use of the term. In the last chapter we read that hell had enlarged herself. No matter how you interpret Isaiah 5:14, one thing is certain: There will be no "bursting hell wide open". Hell is perfectly wide enough to accommodate all the liars, whoremongers, haters and sinners that chose to go there.

Another point that should be made is that there is no place on earth that is as bad as hell so we may as well stop referring to certain places as "hell holes". You might have heard that hell has (hath) no fury like a woman scorned, but that's not correct either. The wrath, pain and troubles of hell will far exceed any anger that has ever been unleashed on this planet. The fact is: hell is such a terrible place that even if a person could "raise hell" he wouldn't dare for fear of the awful consequences. For added emphasis, some people answer questions with an emphatic "Hell no!" While this is rude it certainly beats saying "yes" to a place like hell. Hell is no laughing matter. It was prepared for the devil and his angels and will by no means be a pretty place. Additionally:

- There will be no party in hell.
- Hell will not freeze over.
- Satan will not be in charge in hell.
- Hell is not the opposite of heaven.
- There will be no taking over hell.
- Nobody gets to leave to warn their sinful relatives.
- No one will be able to pray you out of any purgatorial fire.

Oddly enough, this place of everlasting destruction is only mentioned about 54 times in the King James Version of the Bible while the word "heaven" appears over 567 times (not including variations such as heavens and heavenly). It would seem as though God is more interested in enticing us with heavenly reward than threatening us with hell's gloom and doom. In fact, the number one fact and the only important one to remember whether saved or unsaved, Christian or not is this: "If you live right, heaven belongs to you." So why is a fact about heaven at the top of a chapter of *"Facts on Hell"*? The answer is simple: It was never God's intention to flood us with information about hell since it was not even prepared for human habitation. The Bible doesn't give us a clear roadmap and view of the place called hell. It does reference several incidents and historical sites that are supposed to be literal descriptions of hell. As legend, myth and folklore has it, hell is a horrible place. Even Jesus and the Bible depict the state of those who die in sin as a painful and miserable existence.

Some theologians have tried to water down hell's terror. Some sinners have tried to deny hell's certainty and some Christians have often served God in fear of a devil's hell that we know was never meant for them. One thing that we can agree on is this: Hell is simply a place that everyone will soon discover that nobody wants to experience. Here are some additional facts about hell:

- Hell's destruction will last forever.

  2 Thess. 1:9, Phil. 3:19, Heb. 10:39

- There will be conscious punishment in hell.

  Luke 16:19-31

- Hell is a demonstration of God's justice.

  2 Thess. 1:5-10

- Hell is beneath the earth.

  Isa. 14:9, Ezekiel 32:27, Matt. 12:40

Could it be?

Scientists tell us that the earth has an open (hollow) center with a huge ball of molten lava so hot that they cannot even record the temperature. As years go by scientists claim that this hollow fire hole is getting larger (enlarged herself?).

- Hell is a place of darkness.

    Matt. 8:12, Matt. 22:13, 25:30

- Hell is a place of sorrow and pain.

    2 Sam. 22:6, Ps. 18:5, Ps. 116:3

- Hell is a dump – Heaven is beautiful.

- Hell is eternal night – Heaven is eternal day.

- Hell is death & torture – Heaven is rest & peace.

- Hell is banishment from God – Heaven is a new presence with God.

- The word "hell" is used for the Hebrew word "Sheol" as well as the Greek words "hades", "gehenna" (geenna) and "tartaroo" in the King James version of the Bible.

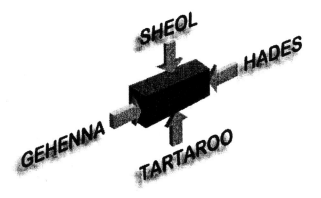

© 2005 By Tentmaker Ministries. All rights reserved

- The words "hell", "grave" and "pit" are all used interchangeably for the same Hebrew word "sheol".

- Many Bibles created in this century do not even contain the word hell in the Old Testament.

- The Greek word "Geenna" was used to describe an actual physical garbage dump.

- The word "Hades" simply refers to the grave in King James' texts such as 1 Cor. 15:55

It is appointed to man once to die then comes judgment. Nobody has to go to hell, wherever it might be, but since repentance and salvation is an individual thing …

We all will **<u>not</u>** be going to hell in a hand basket!

Chapter IV

THE SKINNY ON sATAN

THE SKINNY:

A slang term for inside information; the straight dope, poop or the dirty lowdown.

This chapter is very important. In fact, it cuts right to the heart on why I wrote this book. I want to sound a very clear alarm about satan - the who, the what, the where, when and how. For the most part people are misinformed about him and they are not misinformed in any way that gives them a mental advantage over him. Nobody ever assumes that satan's power is limited. Why is it that people give him the benefit of the doubt? I doubt him. I believe that he is a two-timing, double-talking, lying, cheating, bluffing snake in the grass (no pun intended). I believe that the devil only has one fourth of the power that he has deceived men into thinking that he has. Jesus told the seventy, after hearing them rejoice in the fact that

"even the devils are subject unto us through thy name":
satan has fallen! And I have given you power to tread on the likes of him: scorpions, serpents, and power over all the power of the enemy."

It is interesting that the first word <u>power</u> in the text means authority over all the power of the enemy (Luke 10:19), while the second word <u>power</u> (the power of the enemy) is translated *ability*. So what Jesus is saying is:

"Behold, I give you authority over all of the ability of the devil."

Let's be sure to learn this lesson well. The devil does have power, but we have authority over his power. I want to say it again, a little differently, for the sake of clarity: The devil (satan) has ability, but you have authority over his ability. The constitution of the United States gives each citizen the right to carry and own firearms. You and I are able to purchase and carry a gun if we choose. But if we try to carry that gun into an airport someone with a badge (a guard or policeman) will stop us at the gate. We may have the right and the means (ability), but the guard has been given authority over all of our ability. That's why I wanted to write this book so that the people of God can clearly understand that hell is not in charge! The forces of evil might have the ability to frighten us, hinder us and cause us to experience undo stress. However, we have authority over every thing that he is able to do. This will be discussed at length in chapter eight. We, who are saved and sanctified, must be sure to <u>know our enemy</u>. So here's the skinny on our constant companion: He is one of many disguises and deceptions his name (satan) in Hebrew means *hinderer*. It is his job to hold us back from doing any good, pleasant, or positive things.

The picture of the devil that we all saw when we were kids was probably quite deceptive. The devil is not red and he does not carry a trident (a pitchfork). He comes in all forms at all times and is not a respecter of persons. He hates everybody. He is not a man, but if he were, he would certainly be a misanthrope. He hates mankind and doesn't trust anybody, not even those that love and trust him. Be on the lookout for this crook. You will know him because he will be easy to spot. He's that one in the crowd that's always frowning or sad or causing pain and trouble. He is the one that is never ready for church and never willing to be obedient. You must keep in mind that he is not human. You can't look at your friends and family and call them the devil. They are not the devil. satan might be using them, but they are not the devil. satan was once the highest ranking angel in the heavens, but he got beside himself and became disobedient and downright defiant. This led to him being tossed out of his position and thus becoming the chief enemy of man and all that is good.

You may have noticed by now that I have used his name interchangeably (satan/devil), but these two are just a drop in a bucket compared to some of the names, titles, positions and roles that satan has taken on. The following is a list of some of the more known designators for this vile bag of hot air. Some people make a distinction between satan and some of the following names, but they all either represent him or some of his imps and influence.

- <u>Accuser of the brethren:</u>　　Rev. 12:10

    "And I heard a voice saying in heaven, Now is come salvation, and strength, and the kingdom of our God, and the power of his Christ: for the accuser of our brethren is

cast down, which accused them before our God day and night."

- Power of darkness: Col. 1:13

  "Who hath delivered us from the power of darkness, and hath translated us into the kingdom of his dear son:"

- Prince of this world: John 12:31, 14:30, 16:11

  "Now is the judgment of this world: now shall the prince of this world be cast out."

- Thief: John 10:10

  "The thief cometh not, but for to steal, and to kill, and to destroy: I am come that they might have life, and that they might have it more abundantly."

- Old serpent: Rev. 12:9, 20:2

  "And the great dragon was cast out, that old serpent, called the devil, and satan, which deceiveth the whole

world: he was cast out into the earth, and his angels were cast out with him."

- <u>Murderer</u>:   John 8:44

    "Ye are of your father the devil, and the lusts of your father ye will do. He was a murderer from the beginning, and abode not in the truth, because there is no truth in him. When he speaketh a lie, he speaketh of his own: for he is a liar, and the father of it."

- <u>Tempter</u>:   Matt. 4:3   1 Thess 3:5

    "And when the tempter came to him, he said, If thou be the Son of God, command that these stones be made bread."

- <u>satan</u>:   1 Chron. 21:1   John 13:27   Rom. 16:20

    "And the God of peace shall bruise satan under your feet shortly. The grace of our Lord Jesus Christ be with you. Amen."

- <u>Prince of the power of the air</u>:   Eph. 2:2

    "Wherein in time past ye walked according to the course of this world, according to the prince of the power of the air, the spirit that now worketh in the children of disobedience:"

- <u>God of this world</u>:   2 Cor. 4:4

    "In whom the god of this world hath blinded the minds of them which believe not, lest the light of the glorious gospel of Christ, who is the image of God, should shine unto them."

- <u>Man of sin</u>:   2 Thess. 2:3

    "Let no man deceive you by any means: for that day shall not come, except there come a falling away first, and that man of sin be revealed, the son of perdition:"

- <u>Dragon</u>:   Rev. 12:7

    "And there was war in heaven: Michael and his angels fought against the dragon; and the dragon fought and his angels;"

- <u>Lucifer</u>:   Isa. 14:12

    "How art thou fallen from heaven, O Lucifer, son of the morning! How art thou cut down to the ground, which didst weaken the nations!"

- <u>Roaring lion</u>: 1 Peter 5:8

    "Be sober, be vigilant; because your adversary the devil, as a roaring lion, walketh about, seeking whom he may devour:"

- <u>Great red dragon</u>:   Rev. 12:3

    "And there appeared another wonder in heaven; and behold a great red dragon, having seven heads and ten horns, and seven crowns upon his heads."

- Ruler of darkness: Eph. 6:12

    "For we wrestle not against flesh and blood, but against principalities, against powers, against the rulers of the darkness of this world, against spiritual wickedness in high places."

- Adversary (one who stands against):   1 Peter 5:8

- Angel of light: 2 Cor. 11:14

    "And no marvel; for Satan himself is transformed into an angel of light."

- Wicked one: Matt. 13:19, 38

    "When anyone heareth the word of the kingdom, and understandeth it not, then cometh the wicked one, and catcheth away that which was sown in his heart. This is he which received seed by the wayside."

- <u>Father of all liars</u>:   John 8:44

- <u>Serpent</u>:   Gen. 3:4, 14   2 Cor. 11:3

    "And the serpent said unto the woman, Ye shall not surely die:"

- <u>Beelzebub</u>:   Matt. 12:24   Mark 3:22   Luke 11:15

    "But when the Pharisees heard it, they said, This fellow does not cast out devils, but by Beelzebub the prince of the devils."

- <u>Devil</u>: Matt. 4:1   Luke 4:2, 6   Rev. 20:2

    "Then was Jesus led up of the spirit into the wilderness to be tempted of the devil."

- <u>Enemy</u>:   Matt. 13:39

    "The enemy that sowed them is the devil; the harvest is the end of the world; and the reapers are the angels."

It doesn't really matter what you call him as long as you understand that each of his names are an indication of his character. These names also give us a clear picture of what he wants us to see him as. The most deceptive part of this whole name game that he plays is that he doesn't boast about his obvious weaknesses. He wears all of the above mentioned names as a badge of honor. He likes to be known as the big bad fire breathing dragon with the sharp long tail. Why doesn't he just tell the truth? Jesus saw him falling! So I'm giving him a new name:

The falling one, the one who if we would simply resist, the Bible says he will flee. And what do you call a great big giant fire breathing dragon that runs away (flee) when he can't have his way? I call him a wimp! A lie telling, lowdown, easy to flee magician who uses illusions, rumors, tricks, slight-of-hand smoke and mirror outdated WIMPY tactics on those that he thinks are ignorant.

"Lest satan should get an advantage of us: for we are not ignorant of his devices."

2 Cor. 2:11

And that's his biggest threat – knowledge! He hates those most who are not ignorant. We know his games, we know his plan and we know how to win against him. It's simple: Fear God, resist wimps, know his names and you can identify him in a flash. He is a liar. That means that anything that he has made himself out to be (big, bad, mean, scary) he simply is not! and that's the skinny on satan.

*Ain't nobody mad
But the devil!*

Late 70's charismatic expression.

Chapter V

BEHIND THE SMOKE

AND MIRRORS

"They that see thee shall narrowly look upon thee, and consider thee, saying, Is this the man that made the earth to tremble, that did shake kingdoms;"

- Isaiah 14:16

satan needs help! And I'm wondering which of you who are reading this chapter is willing to give him a hand. What does he need? Well, it's simple: He has led a life of deception. He has made people think that he is a big, bad "better be feared" force to be reckoned with. But people of God all over the world are starting to see that satan is a liar. He has deceived us into thinking that he is more powerful than we are. He has told so many bad lies for so long that he even believes his own rhetoric. John F. Kennedy once said: "A man may die, nations may rise and fall, but an idea lives on." This is certainly true of satan. He has used his smoke and mirror show to spark fear and terror in the lives of countless numbers of people across the globe.

Movies such as *The Exorcist*, *The Amityville Horror*, etc. confirm the grip that this liar has on his prey (mankind). He needs you and me to keep watching these evil films and to keep telling spooky ghost stories. He needs naïve folks who will believe a lie. It's important because if we don't help him he could never keep us in bondage. If we don't help him, he would not be able to keep nations at war. If we don't help him, he could not keep division between churches and family members. Without our assistance satan could never strike fear in the hearts of so many people causing heart attacks and other types of nervous breakdowns. Satan is looking for preachers who will sell out and not preach about the death, burial and resurrection of the Lord Jesus Christ. And most importantly, he wants ministers to stop mentioning him and preaching against his kingdom. Are you willing to help him? I certainly am not! Every chance that I get I am going to remind my brothers and sisters that hell is not in charge by boldly declaring scriptures such as:

- *... greater is he that is in you, than he that is in the world.*
  1 John 4:4

- *... Resist the devil, and he will flee from you.*
  James 4:7

- *There has no temptation taken you but such as is common to man: ...*

  1 Cor. 10:13

- *... we are more than conquerors through him that loved us.*

  Romans 8:37

When we come to realize that satan is a wimp who is depending on us to help him win his shallow victories here on earth, we can lead more prosperous and productive lives. I am sure that this is new to most of you reading this book. It is new because it is rare to hear a gospel preacher call satan an outright W.I.M.P., a <u>w</u>hiny, <u>i</u>nsignificant, <u>m</u>eddlesome <u>p</u>retender. A wimp is actually defined by Webster's New Universal Dictionary (unabridged) as a weak ineffectual, timid person.

Also, in the verb form "wimp" means to wimp out, showing timidice or cowardice; in other words to chicken out. Why do I say that he is a wimp? Because behind the smoke and mirrors is just a magician, an illusionist who plays with our minds in a never ending effort to make us destroy ourselves. His only power is the power of bluffs and fear. If we could see him now as we will see him later we would laugh at him and shake our heads in disgust. Notice what the Bible says about him. This will serve as a point of reassurance for those who do not believe what I am saying. According to the Book of Isaiah, this wimp will soon be exposed for what he truly is:

"How art thou fallen from heaven, O Lucifer, son of the morning! How art thou cut down to the ground, which didst weaken the nations! For thou hast said in thine heart, I will ascend into heaven, I will exalt my throne above the stars of God: I will sit also upon the mount of the congregation, in the sides of the north: I will ascend above the heights of the clouds; I will be like the most High. Yet thou shalt be brought down to hell, to the sides of the pit. They that see thee shall narrowly look upon thee, and consider thee, saying, Is this the man that made the earth to tremble, that did shake kingdoms; That made

the world as a wilderness and destroyed the cities thereof; that opened not the house of his prisoners?"

Isaiah 14:12-17 KJV

You see even the word of God calls him a wimp. You can see it more clearly in verse number eleven:

Isaiah 14:11

"Thy pomp is brought down to the grave, and the noise of thy viols: the worm is spread under thee, and the worms cover thee."

For those who may still not get it let me make it plain. Starting at verse nine (Isa. 9) this evil liar is being taunted: Here's how the New Living Translation says it:

"In the place of the dead there is excitement over your arrival. World leaders and mighty kings long dead are there to see you. With one voice they all cry out, Now you are as weak as we are! Your might and power are gone; they were buried with you. All

the pleasant music in your palace has ceased. Now maggots are your sheet and worms your blanket. How you are fallen from heaven, O shining star, son of the morning! You have been thrown down to the earth, you who destroyed the nations of the world. For you said to yourself, I will ascend to heaven and set my throne above God's stars. I will preside on the mountain of the gods far away in the north. I will climb to the highest heavens and be like the Most High. But instead, you will be brought down to the place of the dead, down to its lowest depths. Everyone there will stare at you and ask, Can this be the one who shook the earth and the kingdoms of the world? Is this the one who destroyed the world and made it into a wilderness? Is this the king who demolished the world's greatest cities and had no mercy on his prisoners?"

Isaiah 14:9-17 NLT

It is fair to note that satan is a very experienced and crafty wimp. Without the power (authority) of the Holy Ghost and the name of Jesus we can't fight him alone and win. The good news is that we don't have to fight him at all. The Bible never told us to fight the devil. All we have to do is resist him and he will flee. If there is ever a time where a fight is necessary, all we have to do is pray and resist. Prayer will summon guardian angels and get the attention of the whole host of heaven and satan doesn't want to deal with angels like Saint Michael and billions related to him. Prayer summons our protective guardians and when satan sees that he can't aggravate us he doesn't wait around. And the reason he doesn't is because as Isaiah 14:9 indicates, he is full of pomp (majestic and magnificent displays). He is the great pretender, but as the Bible has shown, he will be brought down and exposed. Now, I ask you, what does it mean if the <u>head</u> of the forces of evil is nothing but a pompous wimp? I'll tell you ... It simply means that

Hell Is Not In Charge!

Chapter VI
sATAN'S DEVICES

2 Cor. 2:5-11 NLT

"I am not overstating it when I say that the man who caused all the trouble hurt your entire church more than he hurt me.

He was punished enough when most of you were united in your judgment against him.

Now it is time to forgive him and comfort him.

Otherwise he may become so discouraged that he won't be able to recover.

Now show him that you still love him.

I wrote to you as I did to find out how far you would go in obeying me.

When you forgive this man, I forgive him, too. And when I forgive him (for whatever is to be forgiven), I do so with Christ's authority for your benefit,

So that satan will not outsmart us. For we are very familiar with his evil schemes.

"...we are not ignorant of his devices."

2 Cor. 2:11 KJV

Have you ever had a secret that you hoped nobody would find out? How would you feel if somebody not only detected your secret by spying on you but told the news media and the entire world your personal secret? Not a good feeling, huh? Well, that's how the devil feels every time you or anybody reads this chapter. He has some secret evil devices that I am pleased to share with you, the media if they want to hear it, and the entire Christian world. Unfortunately, the evil schemes of satan are way too numerous to mention in this book. He has literally millions of individual devices. The categories range from A to Z and they are designed to cause grief, torment, chaos, confusion, and stress in the minds and lives of the people of God. Since the number of satan's devices is so great, I am going to list a few of the major ones. Once you see how he operates you will be able to detect where his evil devices might be in your life and stamp them out while sending the alarm for others (he hates to be exposed).

Since we referenced 2 Corinthians 2:11, I think it is appropriate to mention first the device that the Apostle Paul brought to our attention.

Device #1 <u>**Non-Forgiveness**</u>

After making an emotional statement about how bad the church was hurt by evil-doers, Paul admitted that he tested the saints' obedience by asking them to forgive a person who may not deserve it. This request was especially difficult since most of the people that were hurt had not fully healed. Healing from personal offenses is a process that sometimes takes years to accomplish. Many go to their graves never fully comforted from satan led attacks that they had suffered. Satan knows that healing takes time as well as positive interaction. James, that great apostle, gave the prescription for healthy reconciliation:

"Confess your faults one to another, and pray one for another, that you may be healed. The effectual fervent prayer of a righteous man availeth much." James 5:16

Paul and James know the power of forgiveness and that positive interaction and earnest prayer has great power and can bring wonderful results. But when personalities and other factors clash, forgiveness efforts often fail leaving us vulnerable and separated (divided) from our own kinfolks, spiritual and natural. Paul added something that makes forgiveness a little easier. In verse 10 (2 Cor.), he said "I forgave him <u>in the person of Christ</u>. In other words he was acting in the authority and in the stead of Jesus Christ. In every difficult situation that we are confronted with we should all ask ourselves "How would Jesus handle this?" After that we should govern ourselves accordingly. Make no mistake, a lack of forgiveness is one of satan's chief devices, so be sure to begin immediately to forgive so that satan will not get an advantage of us, for we are not ignorant to his devices.

"The weak can never forgive.

Forgiveness is an attribute of the strong."

Ghandi

Device #2   <u>Attacking your fruit of the spirit</u>

It seems that the more I watch Christian television and listen to songs by contemporary Christian artists, the whole focus seems to be on blessings, shouting (which usually means partying), prosperity and showing off spiritual gifts. There is very little talk these days about fruit (of the spirit). Nothing makes satan happier than to see a child of God who is devoid of or lacking any visible display of the fruit of the spirit. He likes to see shaky, <u>usable</u> Christians who are tossed about by every wind and doctrine. He does <u>not</u> want us to be like trees planted by the rivers of water that are well nourished, deep rooted and bearing good, healthy, beautiful fruit. Fruit trees in days of old were important sources of providence and nourishment for weary travelers. Jesus frowned on a fig tree that bore no fruit.

"And on the morrow, when they were come from Bethany, he was hungry: And seeing a fig tree afar off having leaves, he came, if haply he might find any thing thereon: and when he came to it, he found nothing but leaves; for the time of figs was not yet. And Jesus answered and said unto it, No man eat fruit of thee hereafter for ever. And his disciples heard it."

Mark 11:12-14

"And in the morning, as they passed by, they saw the fig tree dried up from the roots. And Peter calling to remembrance saith unto him, Master, behold, the fig tree which thou cursedst is withered away."

Mark 11:20-21

Farmers tell us that fig trees grow quite differently than other types of trees. When Jesus saw the tree afar off he expected that it would have at least a few baby figs because the figs (which actually were not due for a couple of months) usually grow before the leaves grow. If there were leaves on the tree then there should have been at least a few baby figs, albeit not completely ripe figs. Jesus was not happy that the tree had a form of fruitfulness, but no fruit.

"But the fruit of the Spirit is love, joy, peace, longsuffering, gentleness, goodness, faith, meekness, temperance against such there is no law."
Gal. 5:22-23

It is the desire of satan to steal, kill and destroy any and all fruit that you might have. He doesn't want you:

1. Sharing love with those who are hungry for care and attention.
2. Spreading joy along with the bread of life which is the word of God.

3. Solving disputes between enemies.
4. Showing or exercising patience while God prepares you to serve.
5. Demonstrating kindness, goodness, faithfulness, gentleness and self-control. These are the only things that are able to prevent wars (as mentioned in the previous chapter) as well as feuds and division.

If satan (like a worm) can kill/hinder the growth of spiritual fruit in your life, he can keep his evil grip on the lives of innocent lost souls everywhere. It is up to us to bear the fruit of the spirit and use our Christian character for the purpose of evangelism. If we don't, it could be that he could get an advantage of us, but we are not ignorant to satan's devices.

Device #3 <u>**Your human nature**</u>

One of the devil's most successful evil schemes is to use your own tendencies against you. He sees you when you're sleeping, he knows when you're awake, he watches you and me like a hawk. He is trying to learn all that he can about us: How we think, how we respond to others in certain situations, what makes us angry and so forth. The definition of human nature is simply the qualities in full that are shared by all humans or the range of behavior that is common for humans to engage in. Without giving much thought to it we know that humans spend their lives dealing with things such as the ones in the following figure.

<u>Figure A</u>

Materialism	Carnality
Common Sense	Sex
Strength	Self preservation
Power	Dependency
Subtlety	Lust/desire

Obviously, the list goes on, but the devil knows that whether we humans approach these things from a positive or not so positive perspective, this is an excellent place to begin, attacking us and our credibility. He likes to challenge our intelligence and test our knowledge of things that God has given us (remember Eve?). The devil is a liar and God has already told us that we are more than conquerors. We, through the power of the Holy Ghost can overcome anything that is set before us, especially as the writer of Hebrews puts it:

"Looking unto Jesus the author and finisher of our faith; who for the joy that was set before him endured the cross, despising the shame, and is set down at the right hand of the throne of God."

Hebrews 12:2

As we look unto Jesus, we can be victorious by following his lead. The Holy Ghost will give us enlightenment which is very much needed because the enemy has had millions of years of practice. We are not alone with the task of dealing with satan's devices, but it takes skill and a bulldog tenacity to hold on to God's unchanging hand and not be ignorant of satan's devices.

With millions of years experience satan has had time to conjure up many other devices and evil schemes. Here are just a few more that have successfully hindered men from seeing Jesus:

- Folklore
- Myths and legends
- Lies and deception
- Religion
- Money
- The love of money
- Covetousness
- Confusion
- All the works of the flesh – Gal. 5:19-21
- Doctrine of devils
- Music
- Peer pressure
- Laws
- Legal rights
- Public opinion

- Gossip
- Media
- Freedom
- Intellectualism
- Education
- High-mindedness
- Ignorance

As you can see, satan has used nearly every facet of human existence against us. Many more devices exist, but again, they are too many to number. It must also be pointed out that some good things can be used as a device if we allow the devil to get his pitchfork in them. All one has to do is read the book of Revelation to see that no matter how crafty satan is and no matter what he devises in the future, we are the winners and he, like his belial suggests, is a worthless loser.

Hell has three gates: Lust, Anger, Greed

- Bhagavad Gita

CHAPTER VII

THE GREATEST LIES EVER TOLD

Benjamin Franklin once said: "A half truth is often a great lie." Not surprisingly satan is not only known for lies, but he specializes in half truths. The following is a list of the greatest lies ever told. Although you may have heard them from some of your friends and neighbors you must keep in mind that you and me (and others) only <u>repeat</u> lies, we do not conjure up lies. The devil is the origin of all lies. Men become liars when they indulge, but lies, half truths, fibs and all other deceptive practices started with satan.

"Ye are of your father the devil, and the lusts of your father ye will do.
He was a murderer from the beginning, and abode not in the truth, because there is no truth in him. When he speaketh a lie, he speaketh of his own: for he is a liar, and the father of it."
John 8:44

The following is just a few of some of satan's greatest and lousiest lies:

Lie #1

Thou shalt not sure die - (first lie).

Lie #2

It doesn't take all of that – (sneaky lie).

Lie #3

Money brings happiness.

Lie #4

What you don't know won't hurt you.

Lie #5

Churches are full of hypocrites.

Lie #6

There is no God.

Lie #7

There is no hell.

Lie #8

Trust in yourself.

Lie #9

God doesn't love you.

Lie #10

Living for God is too hard.

Lie #11

God is holding out on you. Gen. 3:4,5

Lie #12

Man is basically good.

Lie #13

The Bible was written by men.

Lie #14

You've committed an unpardonable sin.

Lie #15

I'm going to heaven because I've been through hell.

Lie #16

I will be like the most high.

Lie #17

It doesn't matter what church you attend.

Lie #18

You can get saved "after" you get your life together.

Lie #19

If I come to Jesus the devil might possess me.

Lie #20

Some lies are harmless.

Lie #21

There are many ways to heaven.

Lie #22

satan does good things sometimes.

Lie #23

I'll make it to heaven since my parents are saved.

Lie #24

God doesn't care about my outward appearance.

Lie #25

God will eventually save/send everybody to heaven.

Lie #26

Churches/preachers just want your money.

Lie #27

What's mine is mine!

Lie #28

Jesus, Moses and Mohammad are all equal.

Lie #29

As long as I don't get drunk/addicted it's okay.

Lie #30

There is no devil it's all fiction.

As you can see from the above list it is utterly useless to attempt to write them all in this or any other book. The important thing is to remember: If it contradicts the Bible or if it came from satan it's a lie.

Rev. 21:8 KJV

"But the fearful, and unbelieving, and the abominable, and murderers, and whoremongers, and sorcerers, and idolaters, and all liars, shall have their part in the lake which burneth with fire and brimstone; which is the second death."

Chapter VIII

TOP 10 REASONS HELL IS NOT IN CHARGE

Obviously, by now it has become very clear that hell is not in charge - not in charge of your life, not in charge of your money and definitely not in charge of your mind. These are things that the devil tries to use in order to take advantage of us. It must be remembered that there is only one reason that satan (hell) wants to be in charge and that is for the purpose of condemning our souls to hell. If you are a saved and sanctified child of God, baptized in the name of Jesus and filled with the Holy Ghost it is neither possible nor probable that you will ever end up in a devil's hell. He knows it and it is the job of ministers and preachers to spread the word. Here are the top ten reasons why hell is not in charge. And remember, hell includes all forces of darkness to include satan. Hell is not in charge, because ...

1. **You don't want it to be (in charge):**
    satan is a liar and a bluff. He has only the power over us that we give to him and only does what we allow him to do.

2. **God is protecting us:**

    Both with a hedge like he did with Job and his angels are encamped about us keeping satan at a safe distance.

3. **You are filled with the Holy Ghost:**

    Although satan may cause you to be sad, down and even depressed at times, he cannot over power the great spirit of God that dwells in you.

4. **You know his tricks:**

    In order for anybody to beat, trick or take advantage of another, they must first have some sneaky tricks up their sleeve. Because you are fasting and praying as well as studying the word of God you are not ignorant to his devices.

5. **He is outnumbered:**

    They that be with us are more than they that be with satan. You plus God is always the majority. Any enemy that knows he is outnumbered will naturally be cautious and sometimes even scared. satan knows he is both outnumbered and outmatched.

6. **<u>God said it (satan is doomed):</u>**

    Every end-time prophecy in the Bible points to the ultimate defeat of the enemy. Death and hell along with satan and his crew will all have their place among the defeated residents of the lake of fire. How can hell be in charge if he has a death sentence?

7. **<u>The weapons of our warfare are not carnal:</u>**

    We may walk in the flesh, but we do not <u>war</u> after the flesh. God has equipped us with the tools (in His word) to pull down all of satan's strongholds.

8. **satan is not omniscient, omnipotent or omni-benevolent:**

   That is, he doesn't love everyone. Since God obviously has these qualities and nobody else does, that places him (God) in charge. No second class evil spirit can be in charge as long as he is in second, third, or fourth place.

9. **We have the victory by prophecy:**

   Jesus not only beheld satan fall at a lightening speed, but he told the seventy that we should rejoice because our names are written in heaven. Could Jesus have been wrong?

10. **It is finished!**

    John 19:30 (enough said)

Chapter IX

HOW TO BE DELIVERED

Just in case you have allowed satan to slip in a little too far into your life, here are a few tips on how to free yourself from the grip of the enemy.

Remember, Jesus died so that we can be delivered from a life of sin. And no matter where you are, the plan of salvation is the same. Repent, be baptized in Jesus' name and be filled with the Holy Ghost. After doing that the only sure way to keep hell from being in charge is to repent. Make a decision and follow it. The decision is to turn from whatever sin, sickness, evil or wrongdoing that satan has tricked you into. Realize and acknowledge that you are in danger. It is also important to recognize that God is looking to save you. He wants to save you more than you want to be saved. If any man, woman, boy or girl would repent daily, hell would never be able to take charge of any part of their life. To repent is to have God-conscious regret, remorse, sorrow, which is followed by a change of mind and action.

In a seminar entitled *"The Scriptural View of Repentance"*, the teacher explained that repentance must be approached from three vantage points:

1) Its importance
2) Its nature and
3) Its demand.

The Importance:

Jesus preached it:	Matthew 4:17
Ministers commanded to preach it:	Luke 24:47
Saints commanded to preach it:	Luke 10:19
John (Baptist) preached it:	Matt. 3:1-2
Peter preached it:	Acts 20:21
Paul preached it:	Acts 20:21
No one is exempt:	Acts 17:30 2 Peter 3:9
Unless man repents he shall perish:	Luke 13:1-3

The Nature of Repentance:

Intellectually (A Change of Mind) -   Matthew 21:29

Emotionally – It is godly sorrow -   2 Cor. 7:7-11

Mentally – It is inner sorrow –   Luke 18:13

The Demand Of Repentance:

Confession of sin –   Ps. 38:17, 18   Luke 15:21/18:13

Forsaking of sin –   Isa. 55:7   Prov. 28:13   Matt. 3:8-10

Turn to God -   Acts 26:18   1 Thess. 1:9

Dying to (from) sin –   1 Cor. 15:36   Rom. 6:3-4

Hell is no match to repentance, basically because the only power hell has over us is the power that we give it. Heaven is always made glad when we repent and satan looses his grip on our lives. Wherewithal shall a young man cleanse his way? The scripture declares that it is by taking heed to the word of God. Your deliverance will come from repentance through preaching (Jonah 3:5-10, 1 Thess. 1:5-10). It will also come through the forbearance and goodness of God which follows true repentance (Rev. 3:19, Heb. 12:6, 10, 11).

Try it and you will soon experience complete restitution. Everything that hell has taken away from you will be returned to you (its rightful owner). You will find a new energy and new relationship with God. You will also become the newest evangelist to spread the good news that ... **Hell is Not In Charge.**

"Then Peter said unto them, Repent and be baptized everyone of you in the name of Jesus Christ for the remission of sins, and ye shall receive the gift of the Holy Ghost."

Acts 2:38

Chapter X

WHO'S IN CHARGE?

Ps. 24
A quick review of the landlord/tenant policy

"The earth is the Lord's and the fullness thereof; the world, and they that dwell therein.

For he has founded it upon the seas, and established it upon the floods."

Ps. 24:1, 2

Apparently, there are some really deceptive devils on this planet that have spread their lies for so long that even humans, (made by <u>and</u> in the image of God) have forgotten the landlord/tenant policy. It is found in Psalm 24 and it applies to every living creature on the planet. Now, we know that <u>hell is not in charge</u> and I don't want to insult anyone with simplicity, but things seem to be getting way out of hand. Truly perilous times have come.

Men have become lovers of themselves, coveting money, boasting about all of their "bling-bling" and material things. They are proud, sacrilegious, and disobedient to God and parents. They never thank God for anything that he has blessed them with. It seems that the world is filled with unloving, unforgiving slanderers who are without self-control. They seem to love pursuing pleasures more than seeking after God. But what does God have to say about man's deliberate attempt to control the affairs of life on his own? The Bible is filled with godly responses to man's arrogance, but none so clear and concise as

Psalm 24:1,2 where God throws the following clause in man's satan-inspired covenant with material things:

Pt. 1 <u>The earth is the Lord's</u>

After all, there is proof in Genesis that he created it (Gen. 1:1). He only gave man charge over a small portion in Eden and he had to evict man back then for breaking the rules and just because you create your own laws and make yourself a title deed to small patches of God's property that doesn't transfer ownership. God retains the title deed no matter what types of rebellion that man mounts up.

Pt. 2 <u>And the fullness thereof</u>

Not only is the land and sea His, but any matter, that is, wood, paper, trees, fish, and other "natural resources". If you eat an apple or fig from a tree in an open field, you are eating God's fruit.

Anything that is formed, found, or fashioned from God's good dirt (matter) belongs to him.

Pt. 3 <u>The world</u>

The phrase "the world" almost literally refers to the part that man is able to inhabit. If man builds a colony under the sea that's God's territory. If man builds a space station on Pluto or Jupiter that's God's planet. Any place that God made and man sets his affection on belongs to God.

Pt. 4 <u>And they that dwell therein</u>

Gen. 2:7 says that God formed man from "the dust". God made dust, God formed a body from the dust, making both the dust and the dusty formation his property, then God breathed (his breath) into his dust and his dust (man) became alive (a living soul). It follows then that no matter how many souls are reproduced by the first soul (Adam), since it was all created and reproduced using

God's raw (dry) goods it all, they all, we all belong to God.

The rules of the house: Ps. 24:3, 4

"Who shall ascend into the hill of the Lord? Or who shall stand in his holy place?
He that hath clean hands, and a pure heart; who hath not lifted up his soul unto vanity, nor sworn deceitfully."

I think the rules are quite clear. If you want the benefits of moving one day to a more upscale part of God's creation, you must:

1. Have clean hands (be honest and fair)
2. Have a pure heart (be honest with God)
3. Not have your soul committing idolatry with material things
4. Not make statements, oaths, and commitments with or for the devil.

For further confirmation of the fact that God owns it all, see Exodus 19:5, 9:29

Now that we have established sufficiently that God is the Lord of the land and we are tenants, let's check the record and see who else (if anyone) claims to own the world and all of its contents. This should be easy since at the time that God made everything there was nobody else around except other pieces of God's created property (angels). God confirms it this way in Isaiah 45:5-8:

"I am the Lord, and there is none else, there is no God beside me: I girded thee, though thou hast not known me:
That they may know from the rising of the sun, and from the west, that there is none beside me. I am the Lord, and there is none else.
I form the light, and create darkness: I make peace, and create evil: I the Lord do all these things.
Drop down, ye heavens, from above, and let the skies pour down righteousness: let the earth open, and let them bring forth salvation, and let righteousness spring up together; I the Lord have created it."

After that, verse 9 begins with a stern warning:

> *"Woe unto him that striveth with his Maker! Let the potsherd strive with the potsherds of the earth. Shall the clay say to him that fashioneth it, What makest thou? Or thy work, He hath no hands?"*
>
> Isaiah 45:9

So you see it is clear that God is in charge! *Any questions?*

Glossary

Adversary — One who is turned against another or others with a design to oppose or resist them; a member of an opposing or hostile party; an opponent; an antagonist; an enemy; a foe. [1913 Webster]

Banishment — to send into exile; to order or prohibit under penalty.

Beelzebub — The title of a heathen deity to whom the Jews ascribed the sovereignty of the evil spirits; hence, the Devil or a devil

Cherubims — An order of angels: a any of the second order of angels, usually ranked just below the seraphim/ one of the winged heavenly beings that support the throne of God or act as guardian spirits.

Compassed — 1. To go about or entirely round; to make the circuit of. [1913 Webster]
2. To enclose on all sides; to surround; to encircle; to environ; to invest; to besiege; -- used with about, round, around, and round about. [1913 Webster]

Complacency — 1. Calm contentment; satisfaction; gratification. 2. The cause of pleasure or joy. "O thou, my sole complacence." --Milton. [1913 Webster] 3. The

	manifestation of contentment or satisfaction; good nature; kindness; civility; affability.
Covetousness	Tending to covet; greedy; avaricious; to want ardently something that another person has.
Doctrinal	Pertaining to, or containing, doctrine or something taught and to be believed; as, a doctrinal observation. "Doctrinal clauses." - Macaulay. [1913 Webster]
Emulation	Desire or ambition to equal or surpass/ ambitious; rivalry; envious; dislike.
Folklore	All of the unwritten traditional beliefs, legends, sayings, customs, etc,
Gallop Poll	A canvassing of a selected or random group of people to collect information.
Gnashing	To strike together, as in anger or pain; as, to gnash the teeth. [1913 Webster]
Heresies	A religious belief opposed to the orthodox doctrines of a church. A church member who holds beliefs opposed to church dogma.
Idolatry	Worship of idols/ excessive devotion to or reverence some person or thing.

<u>Imps</u>	A devil's offspring, young devil/ a mischievous child.
<u>Lasciviousness</u>	Wantonness; characterized by or expressing lust or lewdness; tending to excite lustful desires
<u>Mandates</u>	An official or authoritative command, order, or authorization from a superior official to a subordinate; an order or injunction; a commission; a judicial precept. [1913 Webster]
<u>Misanthrope</u>	A person who hates or distrusts all people.
<u>Pagan</u>	Of or pertaining to pagans; relating to the worship or the worshipers of false goods; heathen; idolatrous, as, pagan tribes or superstitions. [1913 Webster]
<u>Pestilence</u>	1: any epidemic disease with a high death rate [syn: plague] 2: a pernicious evil influence. WordNet (r) 2. Specifically, the disease known as the plague; hence, any contagious or infectious epidemic disease that is virulent and devastating. [1913 Webster]
<u>Purgatorial</u>	Of or pertaining to purgatory; expiatory 1: serving to purge or rid of sin; "purgatorial rites" [syn: purging, purifying] 2: of or resembling purgatory; "purgatorial fires"

Purge	1. To cleanse, clear, or purify by separating and carrying off whatever is impure, heterogeneous, foreign, or superfluous. "Till fire purge all things new." --Milton. [1913 Webster] 2. To clear from guilt, or from moral or ceremonial defilement; as, to purge one of guilt or crime. [1913 Webster]
Reconciliation	A reconciling or being reconciled. Bring into harmony.
Revel	To rebel; to make merry; be noisily festive.
Ruthless	Without mercy or pity; "an act of ruthless ferocity"; a monster of remorseless cruelty" [syn: pitiless, remorseless, and unpitying]
Sacrilegious	Disregard for, or irreverence towards, anyone or anything considered holy, including God, gross irreverence toward a hallowed person, place, or thing.
Seditions	The stirring up of discontent, resistance, or rebellion against the Government in power/ revolt or rebellion.
Subdue	1. To bring under; to conquer by force or the exertion of superior power, and bring into permanent subjection; to reduce under dominion; to vanquish. [1913 Webster]

2. To render submissive; to bring under command; to reduce to mildness or obedience; to tame; as, to subdue a stubborn child; to subdue the temper or passions. [1913 Webster]

Theologian — A person who expounds a specific theology, or theological doctrine.

Vile — Morally base or evil; wicked; depraved; sinful; offensive to the senses or sensibilities; repulsive; disgusting.

Whoremonger — A man who has sexual intercourse or associates with whores.

Bibliography

Boyd, Gregory A. Dr. & Boyd Edward K.; *Letters From a Skeptic "A Son Wrestles with His Father's Questions About Christianity.* Colorado Springs. CO; Zondervan Publishing House, 1984

Dugas, Paul D.; The *Life and Writings of Elder G. T. Haywood.* Portland, OR;
Apostolic Book Publishers; 1984

Foxe, John, *The New Foxe's; Book of Martyrs.* North Brunswick, New Jersey; Bridge-Logos Publishers, 1997

Lewis, C. S. *The Screwtape Letters.* Harper San Francisco, Harper Collins Publishers, 1996

Longman Dictionary of American English (A Dictionary for Learners of English). New York, Longman; 1983

MacGregor, Jerry & Prys , Marie; *1001 Surprising Things You Should Know About the Bible.* Grand's Rapid, MI; Baker Book House Co.; 2002

McNeese, La Monte, *The Top 10 Dumbest Christian Beliefs (Some things don't need to be said).* Bloomington, IN; Author House; 2004

McReynolds, Paul R. *Word Study Greek-English New Testament with complete concordance.* Wheaton, IL; Tyndale House Publishers, Inc.; 1990

Richards, Larry; Every *Good & Evil Angel in the Bible.* Nashville, TN; Thomas Nelson Publishers; 1998

Russell, Jeffrey Burton; Mephistopheles: *The Devil in the Modern World.* Boston; Cornell University Press; 1986

Spence, H. D. M. & Exell, Joseph S.; *The Pulpit Commentary (Volume 16 Mark and Luke).* Peabody, MA; Hendrickson Publishers

Spence, H. D. M. & Exell, Joseph S.; *The Pulpit Commentary (Volume 10 Isaiah).* Peabody, MA; Hendrickson Publishers

Strong, James LL.D., S.T.D.; *The New Strong's Exhaustive Concordance of the Bible.* Nashville, TN; Thomas Nelson Publishers; 1996

The Holy Bible. Nashville, TN; Broadman and Holman Publishers; 1987

The Holy Bible "New Living Translation". Wheaton, IL; Tyndale House Publisher's, Inc.; 1996

The Holy Bible "Old Scofield Study System KJV". New York; Oxford University Press; 1996

Webster's New Universal Unabridged Dictionary. New York; Barnes & Noble Books, 2003

"Hell" Microsoft (R) Encarta; Funk & Wagnalls Corporation1993